Song of Love

NANCY MAY

Print information available on the last page.

Rev. date: 04/07/2015

To order additional copies of this book, contact:
Xlibris
0-800-056-3182
www.xlibrispublishing.co.uk
Orders@ Xlibrispublishing.co.uk

Dedication

This book is dedicated with grateful thanks to my parents, brother and husband, who, during their lifetime gave me the greatest of all gifts – Love.

Contents

A Thought Of Blessing

When we give a thought of blessing it's as though a candle's lit
And the light that passes from it starts a tiny little flame
In the one who takes the gift.
The reflection of this flame within, then re-connects in us
And though it's deep within us, and rebounds without a fuss
In spite of that it's magical, because it reaffirms
That though we may seem yards apart, this really cannot be
If what I give connects in you, then re-connects in me.
It must be that there lies beyond the life that I can view
A bigger life, more glorious than anything I knew.

Communication

Communication is the way that Truth is shown.
It cares not about the words - or music. They alone
Cannot convey the message, for they do not tell the tale.
Indeed, if only words or notes were used then they would fail.
The message lies beyond the words, in gifts that are bestowed
Beyond the sight that we can see, beyond the sounds that flow.
The gifts that are incorporated in the notes these sounds will sing
In music, or in poetry, can sometimes to us bring
A hint of that which lies beyond what we can look and see.
It is this gift, and this alone, that can then speak to me.
If once the heart of Love is touched, the music sings a song
That lies below the words we read, vibrates within myself along.
The chorus then begins, and my heart gladdens once again.
With matching chords within myself, I travel far beyond
What comprehension can teach me. For 'though I recognise the bond
Words must elude my grasp, as in the reverie produced
I'm in Your care at last.

The Universal Mark Of God

The universal mark of God rests on us all.
When we believe that this is so, and our hearts care
For all and everyone we meet
Without compare to what we think should be,
Or want, or think we know,
Then will our actions be induced and fear released,
As revelation of a Love unbounded
Wakes our mind into another state
Where our devotion takes the central stage
And time is shattered in the rising up of bridging Love,
Which takes us on the path to meet again
In Unity and Love within the whole.
For miracles can cut all time to shreds,
And listening to Wisdom from the Source of Love
Will lead us on progression to the Unity within.
Releasing, through His Love, our true direction
To accept the Grace that holds us in His arms forever.
The Golden Rule requires that we believe, with true perception,
That in you and I resides pure holiness, and so we are as one.
Then He Himself can manifest true miracles where e'er we go.
And, though we do not see the ripples that spread out,
We know they do.
For they will spread like water from a tap,
Which spreads in all directions like a flood,
Attesting that wherever we may look lies only good

Glad Song

The song of love is a glad song, at last I know this is so.
I used to think it a sad song and sorrow the path I must go
But sorrow's function I now deny, denial is truly His Way
As I open my heart to His song again, and focus my mind, I can say
A glad song arises from deep within, as the dirge of sorrow I purge.
Fly away, take retreat, you no longer please,
My heart choose again, choose delight.
I have wallowed in darkness yet light now is here
Lift my heart, sweet delight, sing your song.

Gratitude

I'm grateful for the anger and the spite I see around
For only on beholding this will my heart break new ground.
When irritation lashes out, in retrospect I see
A hidden aspect of myself which I would not have be.
In watching it, and monitoring tiny little bits,
I claim the right of Love's return, for it has not left me.
The Holy Spirit's gifts of Love are wiser than my own
And help me through the quagmire, which I wish now to disown.
In tiny little bits He breaks away the solid wall
And never fails to be with me when once I to Him call.
So roll on anger, roll on spite - your power is not so great
I will no longer wallow in the lap of such a state
But step away, and look once more, retrieve the gift of Grace
That comes along when focusing on putting hate back in its place.
In you now lies salvation, in you lies all I am
As I smile away hate's foolishness, Christ's vision blesses me
And Angels bend to touch my heart as peace returns again,
The light of Christ within me reaching out to Christ in you
For unity is Love in form and there is peace reborn.

The Fabric Of Unity

The fabric of Unity lies all around us,
The fabric of Unity tells of His Truth.
When hearts lend their focus
To all that gives blessing,
And search for that meeting point
In all we see,
Then will the weave of His Mantle enfold us
Spread blessings forever to all that we view.
No one can lose when this mantle enfolds us,
Gratitude's song is the call for this gift.
Open, and listen, see all that engages
Only as music, His Heart sings to you.
There are no sorrows, no hurts, no transgressions,
Only our view of them makes it seem so,
But, wrapped with the fabric of Unity round us,
Illusions must fall, for we can to Him go.
Kept in the shades of this weave of enchantment
Let our hearts sink into letting Him Know.

Looking

To search within, while viewing world without
Is but to state that, though we may have doubt,
We have discovered what this world is all about.

Love's Refrain

Love's refrain is all around me if I take some time to see,
A child at play, a haunting song, can reach the heart of me.
I feel the pull of Unity, connectedness the key,
So, on my journey into town, this I'll choose to see.
A mother with her child, whose smile ignites a swift response,
A man who gives his seat away, because he has the choice
To honour one who stands close by, who needs to take a rest,
Her gratitude repaying him for giving of his best.
This tiny act of kindness, using eyes that truly see
Another's needs are part of him, and so it cannot be
That what he gives another can be ever lost to me.
The birds display their love dance on the rooftops on the way
They build a nest, unite, and then again, high in that tree
It could be that I look and hear just squawkings up above
Or, then again, perhaps I'll see perfection in their love.
The parents bringing food to share, preparing well the nest
Returning time and time again to give chicks of their best.
Despite the fact creation in this world is but a lie
Within it still is purity of heart - no need to sigh.
Reminding us we're not alone, our life is not a sham
For still within, though hidden, I do know who I am.
And if I look on giving as a joy and a delight
Then Love will swell within me, give reflection in my sight.
For Gratitude is part of Joy, and Joy is His domain.
So, with a laugh I'll start my day, and pass His message on
That Peace and Joy are His refrain, dwell not on Fear, nor Pain.
Take notice of the thoughts you think, look out for what gives Peace
Throw away Ingratitude - it has no place - Hate cease.
Within ourselves its cancerous, it gives us only harm
Much better then to sing His Praise, and live within His Song.

The Jewel Of Gratitude

This sparkling jewel, this gratitude, what is it? Whence doth come?
It shines a light magnificent, it, miracles hath done.
Each time the light of love is thrown into another's path
The Christ within illuminates, in blessings we both bask.
Each tiny thought of gratitude sends out a tiny shaft
Which penetrates the universe, for that's where it is from.
We little think, with every grin, with joy, we send a beam
Connecting us to all that is, it really doesn't seem
That looking at the beauty in a flower, - or a tree,
Or sharing gifts in gratitude, connects it all to me.
And yet, it must, for Love is there and Love is all there is.
So, in the gift of gratitude Christ's consciousness is shared
And we can learn to dance through life in knowledge all is well,
While letting jewel of gratitude take hold, and in us swell.

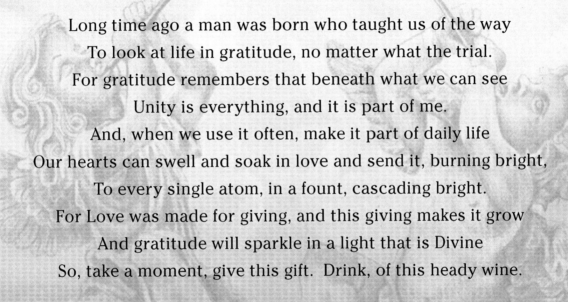

Long time ago a man was born who taught us of the way
To look at life in gratitude, no matter what the trial.
For gratitude remembers that beneath what we can see
Unity is everything, and it is part of me.
And, when we use it often, make it part of daily life
Our hearts can swell and soak in love and send it, burning bright,
To every single atom, in a fount, cascading bright.
For Love was made for giving, and this giving makes it grow
And gratitude will sparkle in a light that is Divine
So, take a moment, give this gift. Drink, of this heady wine.

Healing Georgian Music

Mystical music casts its spell into the air. Three notes
combine, and they delight, for they are fair.
Resonance surrounds us as we sit spellbound, for in the
midst of us there floats a sound, profound.
One voice sings high, another low, while in between a shifting
balancing of notes serene.
The intertwining of both high and low leaves us delighting in
the throbbing flow.
Too soon we have to break this wondrous spell - a short
break, then again hypnotic swell.
To hear the sound is not to tell its power for, within the
singers' hearts there is a flower,
Its perfume spreads its incense on the air and we unite, at the
invite, to share.
When sound and silence intermingle and make one, this
Divine Unity invests the song
With power, to penetrate beyond the veil, and then the boat
of Love sets sail.
A haunting echo of God's Holy Will to end all separation and
at last fulfil
The heartfelt wishes of a lonely child, who trusts, and
follows, and forgets to hide.
Who, wishing unity, unites once more, leaving behind all
worries on the distant shore.

The Buoy Of Love

Into the halls of wonderment and joy my heart will pass

As through the pit of darkness and despair my gaze is lifted,
at long last.

With quickening speed the buoy of love will rise through deep
dark depths of hate,

Which I disguise.

This clingy substance is no barrier to its speed,

for it will pop up,

Reign supreme, on top of waves.

With dark still waters underneath, so very deep, it, on the
ocean's top, will view anew

All that is beautiful, filled with the light of You.

Love – God's Unstoppable Tidal Wave

There is an unstoppable tidal wave which is always in full flow,
Expansion is its nature and it's everywhere I go.
Sometimes I think I see it, often I think I don't.
Sometimes I choose to flow with it, sometimes I think I won't.
But 'though the choice to choose is mine I cannot stop its flow,
For, even if I deny it, it is everywhere I go.
It penetrates the fabric and the weave of all that is,
And the choice is ever present to accept what always is.
Beyond the view I show myself a Garment Royal is spread.
I wish that every moment I could keep this in my head,
That there's nothing there to hurt me and I could choose instead
To take Love's mantle, wrap it round, for that's the way I'm led.
- I may choose to resist it, and sadly, sometimes this I do,
But, always, everywhere that is, Love is there - and so are You.

Another Choice

My thoughts, they are unknown to me, but not to You. This is a paradox I did not know was true

Until you sent Your gift to us once more, to teach us, once again, what life is for.

Our path is made from Love - or maybe Fear, that choice alone we must decide to steer.

If we choose Fear, which masquerades as hate, or guilt, or sorrow, anger too, we state

That in our hearts we've run away from You and we must then decide to choose anew.

Why is our path bestrewn with anguish and with pain? Perhaps we think by this we'll have some gain?

Choose once again and find the Truth in you. The path to Him is never this way lain.

So change your thoughts, reflect without what lies within, and peace will flow, with loss of every "sin"

The Urge To Sing

Within the heart of every living thing, locked deep within, there lies an urge to sing.

Encapsulated in the fibre of its weave a sound vibrates, which cannot ever leave.

And, with this resonance profound, it weaves its way throughout the ether, that our hearts may say

You are the Lord of Light, the One Who knows that through Your Song of Love all Nature grows.

For You have left Your mark in every living cell, so that the listening heart may one day tell

To all the world, the Cosmos sings a song, a Love refrain, in which we all belong.

That, when we seek within and strike this chord, then we will know all things have one accord.

And, in the singing of this note complete will our hearts soar, and we will be replete.

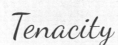

Tenacity

What is this gift tenacity? Is it a gift or curse?

Perhaps it all depends upon the thoughts we choose to nurse.

If sheer intent to get my way, despite the cost to all,

Motivates this attribute, it's nothing but a curse.

If it instead is powered by desire to seek His Way,

To open up the heart to Love, despite what others say,

To act with gentleness and care, to listen, not to judge,

But see behind all outbursts a need for further love,

Then, in tenacity can rest a jewel sparkling bright

That, in its lustre can be found the way back to true sight.

The Inner Star

I seek again that place of silence and intense intent
Where Star of David rises to enfold myself.
Where light of love spreads out beyond the body's shell
And shows another way to see that which I am.
In symbols does Your Thought reveal the way,
In quiet blessings then my heart can say
I do not know, yet You can think for me
So let it be.

Time Trap

When I look back with thoughts of yesterday, I waste my life, for I live now.

With thoughts of future too, I drift away and lose the moment.

The ego then delights, for these are his abode.

His plan, to keep me trapped within the cage of time

And I, like puppet on a string, dance to his tune

And waste away the precious opportunities

To see anew what really is the purpose of my life.

Breathe in the moment, fix your eye on now

And let the mystery of Love break in to sweep away both doubts and longings

And refresh my being with the thought of You.

Then will Communication break right through

And show my heart that I belong to You.

Song Of Love

What is the song of Love? Where does it sing
But in the heart of every living thing.
I cannot know the depth of what You are,
Yet, in Your Wisdom You are near and far.
How can it be that I could hide from You
When every living thing is of Your hue?
There is no place that does not sing Your Name
Nor realise that we are all the same.
This anthem rises as the world gives praise
And gratitude becomes Your sacred place.

Your Wisdom Encompasses All

Though I don't understand all that happens,
Though I don't like the things that befall
Pray, dear Lord give me strength to live daily
And even in sorrow recall
That Your wisdom is greater than mine Lord,
That Your wisdom encompasses all
That whatever befalls is Your doing
May I never from Your grace e'er fall.

Life

This is the place where Time and Space design to meet and intermingle in a web of hate,

To trick our hearts and lead our Mind away into the dream of future or the dance of past,

To tempt us once again to play the fool with twisted longings and deluded thoughts,

To focus on the tiny and the dull,

instead of reaching in to feel the pull

Of all delights that lie within our grasp.

A moment hidden - in a flash revealed - for in God's hands the boundaries that bind

Are broken, and flood our hearts with love of all mankind.

For in His sight are all things seen anew,

the body's reign of power dismissed

And in its place the glory of the shrine that blazes out

and mingles into One

Then do our hearts regain what we thought lost and Peace return to bless us once again.

A Blazing Beam

Through darkest depths of hate
The tiniest glimmer of Your light will shine,
And, from this tiny ray of hope,
A blazing beam may swell.
Only the smallest effort on our part
To make this glimmer take the centre stage
Is what will make this miracle occur.
For, as we turn our gaze upon its glow,
Like air, that fans the dying embers into flame
This radiant light will grow and grow.
And, as it grows old memories will rise
And re-connection to the fountain of our Source
Will push away our troubles,
Fill our gaze with all that You will show,
And, at that time, once more, then we will know
That nothing that we saw before means anything at all.
For, in the light of Love there is recall
That we are more than we have ever thought
And, in ourselves, the light is greater than we know
- A blazing beam -

A Mother's Love

My mother left a gift for me. It's carried in my heart
For though she's dead these many years - we'll never be apart.
The memories I carry were given graciously
By one whose love was always there to help me on my way.
She taught me oh so many things on each and every day,
In little things and little ways, much more than I can say.
She seemed to work so tirelessly and toiled through night and day,
Yet never once did she complain for that was not her way.
With gracious smile and cheerful heart
she journeyed through each day.
Because, within her heart there lay an inner sanctuary.
And though her life was full of toil her heart was full of praise
For, in the people all around she could see His rays.
She very rarely went to church, this - time would not allow,
But, in her heart she'd visit it for, in her heart she'd vow
To place her family and their joy way above her own.

For serving them gave joy to her reflected in her home.
For nourishment is more than food, nourishment is heart.
And when a heart is bountiful the lesson it imparts
Cannot in words be ever told because, within, it starts
Another way of seeing life, a way that Love imparts.
For, when a love is freely given, that love is spread around,
And in that way of looking Love is always found.
So thanks are due to mother's love and this I freely give,
For in my heart she'll always be, we cannot ever part.
Communication is a gift which can sometimes be misused,
But, if in love it's given, it cannot be abused.
For with the selfless offering which mothers know full well
The seeds of trust, of opening the heart to what's beyond,
Are part of this true offering, which leads us to the pond
Of crystal clear acknowledgment of all that lies beyond.
So thank you, mam, for giving me foundation's corner stone
That love is everywhere I look - the way to my true home.

The Miracle Of Love

The miracle of Love lies within me,
In treasure trove, which I have locked away.
Forgiveness holds the key to turn the lock
And make, of every day, a time to say
In you I find my passage home, for I
Have long disguised the path with thoughts of woe.
It takes the miracle of Love to set me free
To find that you, my friend, are part of me.
For miracles deny what judgment tells
And sees instead another way to be.
It sees that if in you I seek out good
I will have found salvation, and I could
Remember, what for eons I have known,
That in myself lies Love, for it must be
That you are part of me, and part of Him.
And in the Song the rays of Love set free
The miracle of Love serenades me.

Calling Out For Love

We all are calling out for Love. Within ourselves we know
There's really nothing else in life to take us on life's flow.
The cries for help, from all around, rise in a mighty swell
For, in our hearts we recognize this power, what it would tell.
It may be that a loved one's gone and sorrow makes us snipe,
It may be that our jealousy makes us take a swipe.
Despite the selfish actions that we all know, very well,
Inside of us there still remains a little voice to tell
That nothing ever harms us, everyone is here to help,
To guide us through our foolishness to betterment and Self.
Discernment can then teach us that all is based on Love,
A call for it, or gift of it, is all that ever is.
We always know, inside us, if the choice we've made is right,
But only in wise choosing will we find a better life.

Extract From Uncle Bill Poem

This poem was given to my cousins after the death of my uncle many years ago and is a short extract from a much longer poem.

Love is like a fountain, gushing from the very soul
The aim of every life should be to make this end our goal.
When loves unite at parting there's fulfilment and release
Emotions soon will quieten and leave your heart at peace.
In times to come that peace on you will shed its rosy glow,
It won't take long for sorrow to depart, and then you'll know
That powerful emotions, once released, leave in their wake
Memories reflections, like a deep and peaceful lake.

Silence

Beyond the realms of time and space
Within, there lies another place.
A place where sorrows fade away
And symphonies of silence play.
Where angels gather in a throng
To add their presence to the song.
This harmony of sweet delight
Pulsates and throbs to dizzy heights
And when, at last, the song does cease
It leaves a reservoir of peace.
Its strains, like music, fade away
Its harmonies refresh the day.

The Inter-Penetrating Weave

The inter-penetrating weave of everything that is
With silken threads of gold and silver spreads
Its iridescent light, and Beauty's sheen,
That in its safety, though oft-times unseen,
All things repose in quiet certainty
That all is well.
Why do we strive to hide from view the truth
And interweave our net of fear and pain?
To fill our lives with guilt, in hope of gain?
Yet what can gain when malice is the source
And Truth is hidden that our truth may guide
And lead us in a tangled web of hate?
Yet hidden, never lost, behind the scene

There waits the web of gold to welcome home
The contrite heart, which seeks to find again
The home of Love.
What need we do to throw aside the shield
Which we erect to hide from us the gleam
That in its warmth and comfort we may yield
And feel the certainty once more of Love?
The secret, we are told, is only this,
Forgive your brother, see in him the truth
That shining loveliness is his, and yours as well.
Let all else melt away, then you can tell
The world that peace again is yours
And Love at last has caught you in its spell.

Invitation

I know You are magnificent and radiate pure light
You stand beside me, throughout time, just hidden from my sight.
You know the very core of me, my essence - pure as gold,
All that is good You see in me, and this You'll always hold.
You cannot see unworthiness, but only sorrow's goal
To reach the treasure deep inside, and once more become whole.
I know You touch me tenderly and resonate pure Joy
I long to throb, along with all, to pulse in harmony
To hear Your voice direct me and answer to Your call.
You are so very close to me, I long to feel Your warmth
To see You stand before me, Beneficence and Grace,
Enfolding me within the Truth reflected in Your face,
Making a re-connection with what has always been
So come, my Love, to guide me, and light my path ahead
Direct me now, unerringly, for I have long here bled.
I would no more be part of this, for I would have instead
The feast of Joy abundant that You hold out ahead.
The time is now to grasp it, and hold it to my heart
So come to me and show Yourself, I would not be apart.

Golden Seed

A tiny little golden seed lies deep within my heart.
Each day it grows, as tender thoughts I to the world impart.
At times my life seems full of tears, but at these times it's true
My gaze will often turn once more to centre then on You.
A golden shaft will, from this seed, spread out o'er all the world,
For You are everywhere that is, and when Your Love's unfurled
It makes connection soul to soul, if I but think of You.
A power, that's far beyond my own, connects me to the core
Of everything that ever was, and opens wide the door.
For this seed knows of unity.   It knows that all is well.
It knows, if growth is stunted, someone soon will come to tell
The way to make it grow again, for it can never fade away
Nor can it ever die
The golden seed of Unity, in furnace only glows
Impurities are burnt away, its sheen glows brighter still
For everything that happens here just takes us straight to Him.
So, just today, have happy thoughts. Release all thoughts of woe
And let that tiny golden seed begin to grow and grow.
Think Unity, think Love of all, remember we are One
Rest in the holiness within of each and everyone.

Inner Truth

I do not know the thing I am, nor what You are,
But in this space my mind reigns free
Inside the universe within
To search and seek and find the answer
In my hidden thoughts, of that which is Divine,
And wise and always kind.
Within me lies the secret of my search,
Within my mind Your Holiness is found.
I know that when You place a thought in me
That it is only so my heart can see Your Love Divine.
Sometimes I "know", beyond what can be seen
Because of You, who reigns within and is supreme.
But though my thoughts may seem surreal
Yet do I know
That they contain the Wisdom of Your Lore
And so, to live in Truth must be my aim,
E'en though it may not seem to harbour gain.
For You must reign above that which we know
And with Your Strength alone must we then go
To Your Domain.

You joined two minds in one delightful day
And glory spread to all, beyond the play
Of those that lie within the circle of our group
For Universal Mind is linked to You
And when we touch, with You, at Source,
Another mind, then is the circle spread
Beyond what we can know,
To aid the spread of all that You hold free.
That gifts shall multiply and shower
The sparkle of Your Beauty to us all.
For we will only share in Truth when we share Unity,
And, when You touch us with this bless-ed gift,
Then the explosion is beyond what minds can think,
And gifts galore must grow, and spread to all that is,
Unless we turn away, refuse to grow
And set our minds in concrete, which is safe and still.
But I will throw this safety to the winds with You
And choose to follow what You bid me do,
Until I grow as You would have me be
And my mind opens, and at last I see
All that is True.

Grateful

I'm grateful for the air I breathe, the sky that smiles above,
For haystacks and the birds that sing, all things, like these, I love.
Beyond the stars that shine above the realms of Love's arms reach,
And when I look up, high above, I know that this they teach.
Let not one moment pass you by, let not one dewdrop fall,
Before you give a thought to Me - for I live in it all.
The colours, vibrant, that I see are echoes of pure Love.
The sunshine on my window pane does not arrest its flow,
Once on the pane it passes through to give each heart its glow.
The smallest insect on my path reflects this light of joy
And even bees and wasps that sting are here to help us grow.
The food I eat, the drink I drink, flows through my body - true,
But thoughts stretch out to those who gave these gifts to me and you.
I hold within my heart all gifts. Give thanks that this is so,
For everyone who meets me now will help me as I grow.
So while I look about me now, and watch the butterflies,
Their wings spread out to catch the sun on this, my windowpane,
I'll cherish that which lies beyond and only this I'll see.
The sun that shines upon me now, the rainfall on my hair,
Convince me that I'm here right now - Can this be right - or be?

Inner Sanctuary

My quiet heart finds sanctuary within the realm within,
And, when I rest between the folds of certainty, all sin
Will slowly ebb away from me. Let then this deep repose
Become the place within each day where I can my thoughts close.
For, when in battles I am locked, when thoughts disturb my peace,
I'll find, that if I run away, my troubles just increase.
But, if I turn my mind, at once, to sanctuary within
I would no longer hold a doubt, no longer look on sin.
For You would wrap Your arms around and hold me in Your calm,
And, in the peace of Your embrace I'll find that soothing balm.
My equilibrium restored, when I return, once more,
I'll have decided, once again, to touch what life is for.
I'll find myself composed again and ready for the fray.
For troubles may seem round about but, having felt His sway,
I will no longer dwell on them, but look on them this way,
I share the light of Love with you, and Peace is now my choice,
With this in mind, the day will pass - I will therein rejoice.

All That Gives Praise

Everything, always , is giving a blessing,
Everything here is only from Love.
Change my perception, so through all my seeing
Only the truth of this, I will then know.
Let not my gaze see the fault that's outside me
But, let me instead see the error within,
For my perception is clearly unfocused
When I, in my looking, see outside me "sin".
Lift up my heart. Let me look with fresh eyes
Let not my cold heart Your message disguise,
But look to the lessons that come to provide me
With new opportunities to search deep within.
To seek out the errors of gross misperception
Forgiving wrong doing, forgiving each "sin".
Only with Love can this looking be focused,

Only self-love gives to others true sight.

Let me then come to You, ask for Your Judgment

For Judgment's not mine - I am far too unkind.

Judgment from You, sweetly flowing, allowing,

Will judge me "Not Guilty" leave sorrows behind.

Lift me up, Father, to dwell in Your Presence

That, in Your Beneficence, I may then gaze,

Watching, adoring the Love that's creating

All that gives pleasure, all that gives praise.

Awaken Or Awake?

Awaken to the joy of who you are
For searching just delays the way to be.
In knowing that your Being is complete
Will fall the happiness to make your life unique.
With Peace and Harmony and Joy within your world
You then can see that only your reluctance holds you back
From knowingness that all is as should be.
What could you need that you do not have now?
For in your inner Being is all there is.
Allow yourself to know that this is true,
As each day dawns repeat this thought anew,
Peace is my home and Joy your Song of Praise
Within myself I can this anthem raise,
For I am always as has ever been
Your holy child, at Home, at peace with You.
And, when I take this thought and hold it true,
You will reveal I am Awake in You.

Sacred Sound

Hauntingly beautiful, melting my heart
The sweet strains of music, within me now start
With touch of soft velvet, its texture most dear,
To call on my spirit to draw very near.
Enfolded so gently within your refrain
My tears fall, in gratitude for His domain.
If I truly listen, then You will draw near
And work deep within me, releasing my fear.
Tears roll down quietly, blessings abound
When listening intently to Your Sacred Sound.
My body then tingles, I sense You've drawn near
Your message, when given, is really quite clear
"Be still. Bid Me welcome. All will be well"
What more than this message can there be to tell?

Peter's Music

Connected and focused, the strings are caressed
And coaxed into giving much more than their best.
Behind the man playing, another, more dear,
Who touches our heart, for this music is clear.
The clarity shared on a level above,
Beyond what we're hearing - far, far, far above.
Another tune playing, and mixing within
The sweet strains of loving and looking within.
The listener unites, and joins in with the sound
And healing occurs, down here on the ground.
True dedication and focused intent
Provide a rare jewel, showing time that's well spent.
Warming the listener, who joins in the song
And lets his heart lift as he travels along
On the strains so delightful, with reverie spent
Tears may arise, but sorrow has gone,
These tears are His blessing for being quite still
Uniting in silence 'til we've had our fill.
Peace is the harmony, Love is the song,
These travel companions can never be wrong.

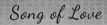
The Sound Of Silence

The sound of silence vibrates in my ear
Its tuneful melody gives ease to pain and fear
Its resonance profound sings songs to lift the flagging heart
And from all worldly cares allows my heavy heart to part.

Meditation

Once more the song of silence sings its sweet refrain
And in its wake it leaves behind a gain
That can't be measured.
In peace and stillness worries fade away
While angel's arms wrap round and gently play
Their touch is treasured.
Quiet heart, held steady, sing your song of love to me
For only in this space in time
Can we unite and see
That all that seems important fades away into thin air
When we in silence pause and wait to feel You really care.
We do not know what happens then,
We only know it does
For unity alone is Love,
In this alone we trust.
For You are in the midst of all
Your light ignites my heart
I know, when I unite with You, we'll never be apart.

Purpose

Unless we have a purpose, we are like a boat adrift,
The power within us, locked away, will not us then assist.
Wouldn't it be better to set purpose at the start,
To know the end of journey, before we then depart?
If we set our sight on ending, believe ending can be now,
We will not have to waste our time in trying to find out how
The task will be accomplished. Purpose set, and held in mind
Will be the answer to the task, for journey we'll then find
Will rest in keeping of the One who knows which way to go.
'Tis our task only to decide if this we want to know.
When once we make our mind up we will set out on the way,
The journey will be effortless if to Him we will say,
"I know that this is what I want. The end is now in sight
Please give to me directions, and give to me Your Light."
It may be that I cannot know how this will yet be done,
But, in knowing destination, is half the journey done.

Blessèd Tears

What blessings fall when we resort to tears
For they have come to wash away our fears.
Sometimes deep sobs will rack our body's form
Tease depth of guilt and sorrow
From what is forlorn within the depth of me.
And tears will surface to release the pain,
As does a cork -pop- to release champagne.
Cathartic and releasing, like a surge against a dam,
To wash away a hidden store of guilt
And with the silt of deep emotion cleanse
And heal, and point a different route to journey
On the way to hope and clarity within the song.
Deep cleansing and deep healing then ensues
And ease, which follows on from tortured flow of heartache,
Is welcomed in with open arms.
At other times, a word, a melody or singer
May touch our depths, and crystal tears
May flow, with heart at peace and in deep reverie.

These healing tears then too are quite profound
For they will give a moment of repose,
A brief connection to an inner world of gratitude and joy.
Like sparkling jewels that catch the play of light,
These tears are crystals that reflect
The hidden depth of Peace and Joy within,
Reminding us, though briefly, that there is no sin.
For in the unity of this repose does my heart sing.
In meditation, too, some tears may fall.
Cool air that opens up the nasal flow
To make connection of a unique kind
Releasing tensions, oft beyond our view,
And blessing us with quiet steady flow
- Deep silence and deep peace -
But yet, I sense beyond this lies another untapped flow
Where tears of rapture will release
Exploding flow of sparkling, joyous jewels upon my cheek,
When re-connected to the depth of Love
And captive in the touch of Heaven's Silk.
This I would seek, perchance at last to know Pervasive Peace.

All

God alone can tell the soul the mystery of All.
Let Silence sing its song of praise let Silence round us fall.
So join as One, and listen well, perhaps this day may be
The day that He communicates all that is All to me.

I Will Know Myself

The time will come when I will know myself for in an instant
am I truly known.
The shackles that now bind must fall away, the seed of Truth
has been within me sown.
All that I am is known to You and so to me for all Your gifts
are given me to own.
What is this life that I would hold so dear except a sad
reflection of my fear?
Above, below and round it surely flows the essence of true
life, and when it glows
It spreads a wave of Love to all that is because Your Will is
everything, and IS.

Prayer

The sin you see lies only in yourself,

Pray not for his forgiveness, for you miss the point.
Only yourself is needful of true prayer,
Only your looking sees a fault without.
Release your prayer from darkness,
Flood your sight with light,
There is no jot of sin out there to see.
No one requires your forgiveness there at all,
When you see error, you make error real,
Yet, how can error heal?
'Tis not the way to find the light of Christ.
'Tis not the key. Only in unity can peace be found.
The purity without may seem to us obscured,
But yet it lies in everything we see.
Take off the patches which obscure the sight
Of one the same: the very self of you.
While, yet, this may not be the thing we view
The Holy Spirit's guidance knows that this is true.
And He alone can make this prayer for you.

Into his hands then, place the judgment. Step away.
Let His forgiveness then, now pave the way.
Ask only one thing, listen, learn and step aside,
Be ye not judge nor jury of what then transpires,
For of this earth this judgment's not a part.
This judgment then will come from deep within the heart
Of God, who over all resides with welcome gift.
Whose purity of sight gives true delight
And over all dominions spreads its light.
Into this flawless Love, this flawless sight
Will the illusions melt away. All will be bright
And unity itself will pulse with joy
Because the Prince Of Peace, through His Envoy
Will clarify the darkness, shine away
All that before could give us some dismay,
And prayer, that song of praise, will rise within,
For in His Gaze will our hearts lift and sing.

Beautiful People

What is it that is beautiful within the folk I meet?
Gentleness and kindness and a nature that is meek,
Not filled with bombast, nor with pride, not filled with selfish whim
But, seeing in their fellow man complete lack of all "sin."
An earnestness when seeking for the treasure that's within
And focus on the love of God, that makes of life a hymn.
Viewing, in their daily life the sacredness of all
And gently walking on their path, while trying to recall
That, though the day is trying, though there's chaos all around
Within their centre peace is found, for all is holy ground.

Man And Wife

When a man has a nature that's sensitive, gentleness
flows from his heart,
If his gaze is then centred on sacredness he will have
many gifts to impart.
To his wife he will offer up everything, the sun, stars,
and sky up above
For, in her, he'll see only her Innocence, Holiness,
Purity, Love.
His blessings he'll pour out upon her, with gentle
caress, her he'll bless.
While under deft touch she will yield to him, uniting in
true holiness.
Bodies then act as a medium for that which pours down
from above
When the focus of meeting is sacredness, the product
produced's Divine Love.

Life Is A Canvas

Your life is a canvas, on which you must paint
Your day to day doings, to access the gate.
That gate, deep within you, well hidden away,
Which holds your dark secrets, your well hidden hate.
But, if you look over the canvas and see
That all that's before you just leads you to Me
That, by looking outward, you view what's within,
Have rare opportunity to throw away "sin"
You then will paint pictures of quite different hue,
For I will have given you thoughts that are true.
With thoughts of Forgiveness, Purity, Light,
Into your looking will pour a new sight
To brighten the canvas, to banish the haze,
For onto your life with detachment you'll gaze.
The pictures before you, though dark they may seem,
Have hidden behind them a glorious gleam.
Detachment, allowing what's there to play out,
Will open your heart wide, to view what's inside.
Quietly knowing life's not what it seems
Allows God's intention to glimmer and gleam.
So, set to your canvas, paint it with glee,
In knowledge , eventually, Him you will see.

A Tiny Pebble

A tiny pebble that is cast into a pond can send out
ripples that do long expand,

And each of us, each day, do ripples spread, because of
thoughts we hold within our head.

Remembering we interact with All, will help us see

That we must leave decisions up to You so that the
Song Of Love will sound notes true

And Glory, far beyond the things we know, will cast its
glow upon us, so that at last we'll know

That we are as He made us, pure and whole, part of His
Infinite Domain, at Peace, at Home.

That Other Realm

My mind will wake, and realize

That what I thought, so long ago,

Was just a tiny glimmer of uncertainty,

That could not long remain

Within the tapestry of Beauty

That is boundless and unlimited

And the essence of Your Love Domain.

For I have spent more time

Than I could wish to own

Within illusions spell, my own refrain,

Which I have wished to drown the Song of Love

And implement, instead, unsteady gain,

That really is but nothingness at all.

I cannot ever from Your True Grace fall,

And, if I hold this thought within my mind,

Then You will come to show me that unkind

And foolish thoughts, are only smoke

To hide the warmth that Fire of Love will show.

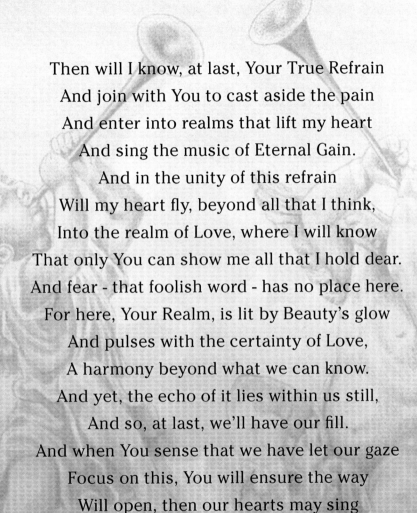

Then will I know, at last, Your True Refrain

And join with You to cast aside the pain

And enter into realms that lift my heart

And sing the music of Eternal Gain.

And in the unity of this refrain

Will my heart fly, beyond all that I think,

Into the realm of Love, where I will know

That only You can show me all that I hold dear.

And fear - that foolish word - has no place here.

For here, Your Realm, is lit by Beauty's glow

And pulses with the certainty of Love,

A harmony beyond what we can know.

And yet, the echo of it lies within us still,

And so, at last, we'll have our fill.

And when You sense that we have let our gaze

Focus on this, You will ensure the way

Will open, then our hearts may sing

In Exaltation as we drink our fill.

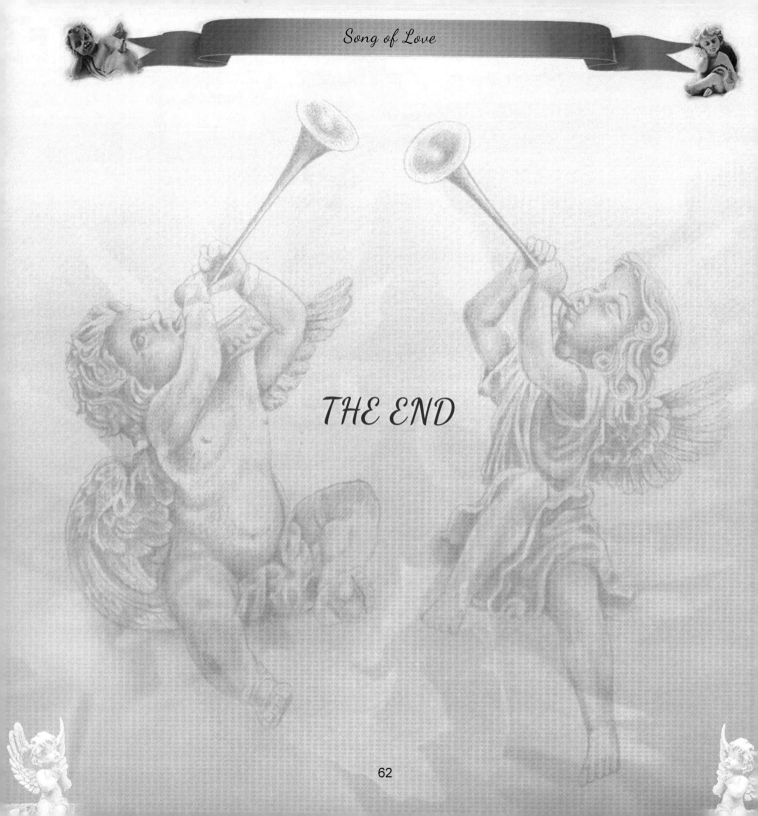

THE END

Edwards Brothers Malloy
Oxnard, CA USA
April 29, 2015